DEALING WITH
DIFFICULT PEOPLE

00165686

CHRISTINA OSBORNE

STRODE'S COLLEGE
★ LIBRARY ★

KT-215-147

LONDON, NEW YORK, MUNICH,
MELBOURNE, AND DELHI

Senior Editor Jacky Jackson
Senior Art Editor Sarah Cowley

DTP Designer Rajen Shah
Production Controller Michelle Thomas

Managing Editor Adèle Hayward
Managing Art Editor Karen Self

Produced for Dorling Kindersley by

COOLING BROWN
9–11 High Street, Hampton
Middlesex TW12 2SA

Creative Director Arthur Brown
Senior Editor Amanda Lebentz
Designer Caroline Marklew
Editor Lorraine Turner

First published in Great Britain in 2002
by Dorling Kindersley Limited, 80 Strand
London WC2R 0RL

A Penguin Company

Copyright © 2002
Dorling Kindersley Limited
Text copyright © 2002
Christina Osborne

All rights reserved. No part of this publication
may be reproduced, stored in a retrieval
system, or transmitted in any form or by any
means, electronic, mechanical, photocopying,
recording, or otherwise, without the prior
permission of the copyright owner.

A CIP catalogue record for this book is available
from the British Library

ISBN 0 7513 1289 4

Reproduced by Colourscan, Singapore
Printed and bound in Hong Kong by Wing King Tong

See our complete catalogue at

www.dk.com

CONTENTS

ASSESSING YOUR OPTIONS

WORKING FOR
CO-OPERATION

DEALING WITH
CONFLICT

INTRODUCTION

The ability to lead difficult individuals out of unproductive situations to improved performance and better working relationships is an essential management skill. Dealing with Difficult People equips you with proven techniques and strategies to enable you to anticipate problem people, stop trouble from escalating, and help awkward staff to become fully contributing members of the team. Find out how to handle difficult people successfully by developing vital observation and communication skills, avoiding confrontation, working for co-operation, and resolving conflict. A self-assessment questionnaire enables you to measure your skill level and identify areas for improvement, while 101 tips offer practical guidance and advice. This book is an invaluable reference for anyone – from project leader to senior manager – who has responsibility for leading a team of one or more colleagues.

UNDERSTANDING DIFFICULT PEOPLE

Difficult people stop us from achieving our goals. Understanding why people are difficult helps you to anticipate who will be difficult and take action to prevent problems and reduce conflict.

IDENTIFYING DIFFICULT PEOPLE

People who are difficult absorb your time and energy. The earlier you can identify who will be difficult and when, the better your chances will be of dealing with them successfully. In order to do this, you need to know what makes people difficult.

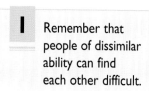

1 Remember that people of dissimilar ability can find each other difficult.

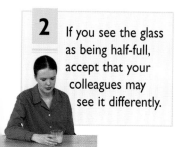

2 If you see the glass as being half-full, accept that your colleagues may see it differently.

UNDERSTANDING WHY PEOPLE ARE DIFFICULT

We all react differently to pressure, and we all have different expectations in life. Sometimes we may find it hard to deal with someone who has a different set of internal values to our own. By understanding ourselves and other people better, we can learn not to judge others because of our differences, to stop trying to change them, and instead to value what they bring to us.

IDENTIFYING WHO COULD BE DIFFICULT

It is possible to anticipate who is most likely to become difficult at work in two ways: from observing people's behaviour in the workplace and from your own personal knowledge of them. Are your employees clear about what is expected of them? Are they able to keep their work and home lives balanced? When you know your staff well, it is possible to avoid difficulties when pressure points arise because you can prepare in advance to offer appropriate support and development in the workplace.

3 Watch for signals that more job variety is needed.

4 Get to know your staff so that you are aware how best to help them.

5 Build a supportive culture and recognize supportive staff.

▼ **RECOGNIZING WHY STAFF BECOME DIFFICULT**
Employees can become demotivated and resentful as a result of poor management. An employee who continually works long, unsocial hours or who feels undervalued is likely to feel dissatisfied, which can lead to their becoming difficult.

ANTICIPATING PROBLEMS

By spotting recurrent patterns of stressful situations at work, you can reduce events in the workplace that trigger stress and prepare yourself for dealing with people who might become difficult. If employees are worried about changes to their job or rumours about redundancy, for example, insecurity and fear may push them into doing the very thing that can work against their future. You should look at your own management style as well as how you are organizing work, reviewing objectives, and developing a supportive culture, in order to prevent people becoming difficult through no fault of their own.

Job insecurity

Unclear objectives

Constant pressure

Lack of job variety

Unpredictable hours

Insufficient workload

Heavy workload

KNOWING HOW PEOPLE ARE DIFFERENT

People with different perspectives bring complementary skills to any group working together. Different perspectives can also cause conflict, however, so you need to understand individual differences if you are to deal with difficult people successfully.

6 Identify team members' skills in order to allocate them suitable roles.

7 Pick a team with varied skills to ensure harmony.

8 Know your team members' strengths and weaknesses.

EXPLAINING DIFFERENCES

People have different ways of learning. Those who are action-orientated learn best from being involved, challenged, and doing a job, while those who are more reflective are thoughtful, cautious, and good listeners. People who enjoy developing models of the world like looking at ideas or theories, while practical people enjoy learning by trial and error, suggesting quicker ways of doing things, and receiving feedback on their latest initiative. None of these people intends to be difficult. They just have different ways of looking at things.

VALUING DIFFERENT PERSPECTIVES

In any team, it is useful to have people with preferences for different ways of learning. An action-orientated member will enjoy dealing with short-term crises and performing a variety of tasks, whereas a reflective member will prefer to base decisions on data and help the group to review actions. The member with a theoretical style will draw up guidelines for action, while the person who prefers experimentation will be impatient to put ideas into practice.

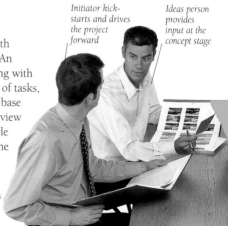

Initiator kick-starts and drives the project forward

Ideas person provides input at the concept stage

IDENTIFYING LEARNING TYPES AND THEIR JOB SKILLS

LEARNING TYPES	JOB SKILLS
ACTION-ORIENTATED This type of individual likes to be fully involved, and is a visible team member who learns through experience.	● Dealing with a variety of work. ● Undertaking tasks with a short-term payoff. ● Challenging projects.
REFLECTIVE This type likes to be able to think about experiences and learns by observing, analyzing, and reflecting on what has happened.	● Research, preparation, and reading. ● Producing reports. ● Reviewing opportunities.
THEORETICAL This team member gathers and reviews ideas, concepts, and principles, and learns by integrating these into a framework for action.	● Setting objectives and developing systems. ● Teaching others. ● Analyzing best practice.
PRACTICAL This type of individual likes to test out principles in practice and learns by trial and error.	● Drawing up action plans. ● Suggesting short cuts. ● Coming up with solutions to problems.

▼ **UTILIZING TEAM SKILLS**
Successful teams have members with the different skills needed for projects. As a manager, you should set clear objectives to ensure that everyone's talents are utilized.

Expert helps to plan and provides technical insight

Networker explores opportunities and gathers resources

BEHAVING LIKE ADULTS

People are thought to approach the world from the perspective of the parent (who assumes that blame lies with the other person), the adult (who assesses situations logically), or the child (who feels he is to blame when a problem arises). Most people switch constantly between these viewpoints. Problems arise when someone communicating from one of these perspectives receives a response from someone with a different one. The miscommunication can lead to angry, upset, or withdrawn behaviour.

 9 Work to change people who always respond negatively.

THINKING ABOUT PEOPLE'S MOTIVATION

Managers need to understand what motivates difficult team members and their own role in motivating or demotivating them. Use this understanding to meet team members' needs and reach your personal goals by achieving the goals of the team.

10 Identify approaches that motivate the team and use them more often.

11 Motivate a difficult person by understanding what they need.

IDENTIFYING INDIVIDUAL MOTIVATION

Team members work most effectively when they feel motivated, and become difficult when they are not. Be aware of the different ways in which people in your team are motivated, and recognize that not everyone will respond to the same reward. You need to identify which of your actions motivate the different individuals in your team, and which are demotivating, in order to enhance your team's effectiveness.

BEING AWARE OF NEEDS ▼
It is important to match your actions to the needs of each team member, so get to know what motivates each person.

Team member is motivated by being given more responsibility

POSITIVE MOTIVATION

Team member dislikes flying and is demotivated by travel invitation

NEGATIVE MOTIVATION

MOTIVATING YOUR TEAM

Give clear direction on team aims and agree objectives with team members. Most people need a sense of achievement, and do not enjoy failing to meet objectives, so identify individual needs for training to reach the required standards. Many people welcome more responsibility when it gives them more control over their work and how it is done. Managers who support and encourage people to work together, and show appreciation for work well done, create team spirit and team members who motivate each other.

Places trust in people

Collaborates with staff

Is loyal to colleagues

Commits to work

Avoids "office politics"

A MOTIVATIONAL MANAGER

THINGS TO DO

1. Greet everyone you work with each day.
2. Go on walkabouts, ask questions, and listen.
3. Remember to praise people if you want them to repeat something.
4. Be inclusive and ask for input to decisions that affect the team.
5. Be consistent.
6. Share information and learning.
7. Coach people to develop their performance and learn new skills.

◀ **ASSESSING QUALITIES**
There are several important qualities that a manager needs to possess in order to motivate staff effectively. If any one of these qualities is absent, staff will quickly lose their motivation.

12 Make people feel that they are part of a winning team.

13 Celebrate good news and team achievements.

AVOIDING DEMOTIVATION

People do not like working inefficiently, having no control over the pace of their work, or being continually under pressure. A manager needs to be aware of the team's workload and what support individuals need in order to do their job well. If objectives are unclear and people are uncertain about what is expected from them, they can appear difficult when they do not take action or do the wrong thing. Managers should communicate and let people participate in making decisions about their roles and the way they carry out their jobs.

UNDERSTANDING THE DYNAMICS

Effective communication moves relationships forward and helps people to work together successfully. By identifying the barriers to good communication, managers can maximize the potential of their team and mobilize difficult people.

> **14** Know that how you communicate is as vital as what you communicate.

SHARING INFORMATION

> **Check that the information is accurate**

> **Decide who should receive the information**

> **Choose the best method of communication**

> **Decide who should communicate the information**

> **Check that the information has been received and understood**

> **Follow up to see whether action has been taken**

ENERGIZING COMMUNICATION

Managers need to encourage a positive approach to communication between team members so that they support each other and become more effective as a team. Behaviour that supports good communication includes offering help, showing an interest in individuals, and acknowledging the contribution each team member makes to the team. Be honest with each other, take the time to explain why things need to happen, and share information. Being clear with the messages you send, and choosing the best way to provide information, will help the recipient to understand your meaning. Developing a positive atmosphere encourages open discussion, creates energy, avoids misunderstanding, saves time, and builds working relationships that are supportive and rewarding.

> **15** Be aware that when messages travel through a long chain of people, they can become distorted.

COMPARING COMMUNICATION ENERGIZERS AND BARRIERS

ENERGIZERS

- Being clear about why you are communicating.
- Thinking how your message will be received.
- Promoting open discussion.
- Encouraging people to listen to one another.
- Questioning to understand the other person's view.
- Showing an interest in what others have to say.
- Acknowledging others' input.
- Summarizing to clarify understanding.
- Building relationships by keeping channels open.
- Providing a supportive, encouraging environment.

BARRIERS

- Being unclear about purpose of communication.
- Presenting communication poorly.
- Choosing the wrong method (for example, writing a message when it should have been delivered face to face).
- Having a hidden agenda when communicating.
- Allowing strong emotions to block the message you are sending, or receiving.
- Deliberately misinforming or sabotaging information.
- Failing to provide clear channels for communication.
- Operating in a poor environment, (noise, dim lighting, etc.).

DEVELOPING EFFECTIVE COMMUNICATION

It is important to look at the channels of communication within and outside the team. Messages should be delivered directly, rather than passed down a long chain, and all team members should be told what they need to know. Any team member who feels excluded from vital knowledge may become difficult and obstruct the team's progress. Really difficult people may even sabotage a team by giving wrong information or delaying action. If a manager allows any strong negative feelings between team members to grow, a spiral of negative behaviour can quickly demoralize the team. As a result, some people may become manipulative, others may withdraw, they will not listen to each other, and the team will become demotivated and ineffective.

QUESTIONS TO ASK YOURSELF

Q Is information being shared in the most effective way?

Q Are the team clear about their goals?

Q Do I welcome ideas and take the time to listen?

Q Do I involve people in making decisions?

16 Always be positive and constructive when you are communicating.

13

OBSERVING DIFFICULT PEOPLE

Observing when people are about to become difficult, and having some insight into what their reasons might be, enables you to pre-empt them. Take the opportunity to turn potential conflict into an exchange of understanding and co-operation.

17 Learn to identify signs that people are about to become difficult.

18 Show people that you value their contributions.

WATCHING BEHAVIOUR

If someone suddenly becomes more difficult, irritable, or angry than usual, this could be a sign of emotional stress. If an individual seems depressed, frequently tearful, or just unhappy, you can gently give feedback on how he or she appears to you and ask how things are going. If the problem is personal, then you can suggest different sources of external advice. Individuals become difficult when they have lost the ability to feel or care through too much stress. Physical symptoms such as an upset stomach and indigestion, neck or chest pain, and visual disturbances can be signs of stress; some people may become difficult rather than admit to feeling unwell or under stress.

RECOGNIZING SIGNS OF STRESS ▼

Keep a watchful eye for signs of stress in the people you work with. Some of the more common symptoms include a quick temper, a decline in personal appearance, lack of concentration, and fatigue.

19 Define roles to reduce competing or defending within the team.

OBSERVING FELLOW WORKERS

MANAGER
As a manager, you should observe whether team members are protecting responsibilities they have acquired rather than completing tasks. Build trust between team members by defining goals and sharing views openly.

SUPERIOR
Hovering, asking questions, or going to others for information are signs that a boss is not being kept informed. You need to give more feedback on progress.

PEER
If someone is tense or concerned, ask if anything is wrong when you are alone together. Be supportive in meetings and encourage the colleague's contribution.

OTHER TEAMS
If colleagues are adopting a them-and-us attitude, improve communication by ensuring that both groups review areas where their responsibilities overlap.

OBSERVING CUSTOMERS

If you take your customers for granted, then even your long-standing clients may leave to go to a competitor. Find out how much involvement and feedback your customers need. Most customers do not enjoy complaining, but if you do not give them what they expect they will take their business away. Customers who do stay might become demanding due to a build-up of disappointment. Check that everyone in the team understands your organization's customer service standards and give recognition to those who deliver customer service well.

20 Encourage team members to focus on customer needs.

Team member listens attentively, noting concerns raised

Customer makes a complaint

SEEKING FEEDBACK ▶
Ensure that staff use meetings with customers to observe and listen to their views on the service being provided. If they seem demanding, find out why, and take action to deal with their concerns.

Managing Different Types of Difficult People

Type of Person	How to Manage Them

Slumper
Has no enthusiasm, sighs, shrugs, but will never say that anything is wrong.

- Encourage this type to reflect on their achievements as they progress towards goals.
- Give praise when due, and check that positive feedback outweighs the negative.

Dumper
Offloads tasks, especially the worst ones, and dumps them on others.

- Set clear objectives, project milestones, and deadlines.
- Draw up an action plan and ensure that their initials are shown against most of the actions.

Jumper
Has no scruples; takes credit for others' work to move up the career ladder.

- Make sure that people who are responsible for projects deliver feedback themselves.
- Define responsibilities clearly and give credit to everyone involved in projects.

Grumper
Complains constantly about every small thing and is impossible to please.

- Hold a one-on-one meeting and ask questions to pinpoint specific problems.
- Ask them to prioritize their workload and set deadlines for achieving objectives.

Bumper
Takes the kudos when all goes well but blames mistakes on others.

- State responsibilities clearly.
- Set stretching targets.
- Meet regularly to review progress against measurable objectives and give feedback.

Trumper
Always has to have the first and last word and be one step ahead of everyone else.

- Confirm in writing whatever has been agreed.
- Have an agenda for meetings, anticipate the objections a "trumper" will raise, and prepare questions and goals to challenge him or her.

Thumper
Bullies and intimidates others and gets his own way by being aggressive.

- Stand your ground by being assertive.
- State your case calmly and ask questions to encourage the person to consider the consequences of their actions.

WORKING WITH PROFESSIONAL ADVISERS

Your professional advisers can add value by giving an objective perspective on you and your team. Observe how sensitive they are to any defensiveness in you or your team members when they are asking questions at the beginning of the project. They may be asking some questions to test how realistic you are being in your expectations. This gives you an opportunity to clarify your objectives and ask yourself what you need from the advisers. Notice how well they observe and how quickly they pick up issues as well as facts.

21 Brief advisers on the potential impact of their work on your business.

22 Be prepared to be questioned by a good adviser.

23 Be open with your suppliers and inform them of your future plans.

MONITORING SUPPLIERS

If you observe that your suppliers are becoming difficult, could it be due to something you have inadvertently done or omitted to do? Issues often arise over payment, and it is very important to have agreed, at the beginning of the working relationship, the levels of service you expect and the terms within which you will pay. Your suppliers need feedback if their service level drops in order to give them the opportunity to improve. Developing good working relationships with suppliers means they will be more likely to help you out when things become difficult.

OBSERVING YOURSELF

As a member of a team, you have to keep a balance between the tension of wanting to excel as an individual with the need to be a fully contributing team player. Observe yourself to make sure you are balancing your development as an individual with your work in the team. Continue to deliver the work you have taken on and make sure you share knowledge with the rest of the team members so that you are, collectively, more effective.

QUESTIONS TO ASK YOURSELF

Q How do other team members regard me as a colleague?

Q How often do I ask for feedback from my team?

Q What skills and strengths should I build and what are my main areas for development?

ASSESSING YOUR OPTIONS

Dealing with a difficult person successfully requires objective analysis and assessment. Consider all your options before choosing the best way to achieve co-operation and change.

PLANNING TO OVERCOME PROBLEMS

You need to understand a problem before you can decide what to do about it. Knowing how to generate and choose the best option and test possible solutions will help you to plan the way forward in order to be one step ahead of a difficult person.

24 Gather as much information as possible to analyze the real problem.

QUESTIONS TO ASK YOURSELF

Q Why is this person being difficult?

Q Is this a situation that has happened before and if so, what caused it?

Q What can I do to resolve this situation and prevent it from happening again?

DEFINING WHY THE PROBLEM IS HAPPENING

Before you can find a solution to prevent someone being difficult, you need to define why the problem is happening. Look at the situation and notice small signs of difficult behaviour. Think about questions to ask. Identify people who have been involved with this person in similar projects before. They could help you review what happened previously and assess how the situation might develop.

GENERATING OPTIONS

There is usually more than one solution to a problem and you need to choose the best option. Approach the problem with an open mind, then look at it from as many different perspectives as possible, including that of the difficult person. You must be prepared to take risks to solve problems, so suspend your judgment for a while and see what happens. Each possible solution could be captured on a post-it note, or you could use images and colours in order to create a picture on a flipchart. Use your imagination to stimulate new and different ideas for overcoming the problem.

POINTS TO REMEMBER

● A problem must be defined correctly before solutions can be developed.

● Information gathered when exploring and analyzing a problem will be invaluable later when looking at possible solutions.

● Some of the best ideas come from involving others in the creative process.

● All possible solutions should be listed before evaluation starts.

TESTING SOLUTIONS

Define the main objectives a solution should achieve

↓

Score solution on how well it will achieve objectives

↓

If solution scores well, identify the risks involved

↓

Generate ideas to minimize or prevent effect of risks

↓

With contingency plans in place, assess if risks are worthwhile

CHOOSING BETWEEN POSSIBLE SOLUTIONS

The best way to make a decision and choose between several options is to think about the criteria against which the final solution will be measured. What objectives should the solution to the problem achieve and which are most important? Prioritize objectives in order of importance. Score the solutions against each objective to see which gets the highest score out of 10. High marks against the most important objectives identify your best solution. Having thoroughly analyzed the situation, and come up with the solution to achieve important objectives, gives you confidence to tackle a problem with even the most difficult person.

◀ **FINDING THE RIGHT SOLUTION**
Narrow your list of options by giving each solution marks out of 10 for how well it achieves objectives. The highest score will suggest the best solution.

AVOIDING CONFRONTATION

When timing is not right, or the costs of confrontation are too high, avoiding confrontation with a difficult person may be an appropriate option. Understanding how to avoid confrontation enables you to choose the best response at any given moment.

25 Recognize that difficult behaviour can become a habit if not tackled early.

26 Be aware of your own emotional response.

27 Give yourself time to look objectively at a situation.

WALKING AWAY

If the difficult person is shouting at you, then there is little point in continuing to try to talk. If the person is too upset or angry to listen, then sometimes it may be wiser to walk away. This gives an opportunity for angry feelings to subside and for you to think through how best to tackle the problem objectively. If you suspect that you are postponing tackling the problem, however, then either determine to deal with it immediately or make an appointment to meet with the other person at the earliest date possible.

WORKING ROUND A DIFFICULT PERSON

If everyone else in the team is co-operative and works well together, it is tempting to work round the difficult person. This could, however, be the wrong thing to do because, by working round that person, you are, in effect, rewarding his or her difficult behaviour. If you need to get something done in a hurry, then once or twice it might be expedient to ask someone else to do the work, but if it happens again it means a precedent has been set. The difficult person may then be regarded as not being part of the team, and so not sharing the same responsibilities, which has a poor effect on the rest of the team.

CULTURAL DIFFERENCES

Britons, Americans, and Europeans may find it difficult to discern whether someone from a more reticent culture has been offended or is not going to co-operate. In Japan, for example, it is important to check whether someone is happy with a course of action or is just being polite, because their body language is different and less easy to read.

LOOKING THE OTHER WAY

Pretending not to notice the bad behaviour of a difficult person may work if that person wishes to remain part of the team. Withdrawing your eye contact can indicate your disapproval of what is going on. Sometimes this is enough to signal that the behaviour is unacceptable and needs to change. If, however, the bad behaviour continues, then ignoring it allows the individual to behave in an uncontrolled manner and this will distance him or her from the team. In some cases, looking the other way will cause that person to become more difficult as a way of regaining your attention. Avoidance tactics may work once or twice in the short term but are not a successful long-term strategy.

POINTS TO REMEMBER

● Any kind of confrontation in an open meeting should be avoided whenever possible. Discussion can be encouraged afterwards.

● In order to avoid antagonizing a difficult person, an open body posture should be maintained.

● Looking down at your notes can help you avoid a hostile gaze.

● Turning your attention to someone else can discourage an individual intent on talking at you.

28 Bear in mind that avoidance tactics are a short-term solution.

▼ USING AVOIDANCE TACTICS

Working closely with co-operative team members and ignoring a difficult colleague can move a situation forwards. Either the difficult team member will join in, or he will move away totally, in which case confrontation at a later date becomes inevitable.

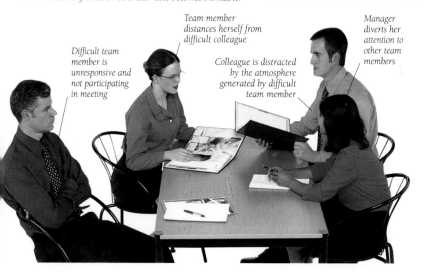

Team member distances herself from difficult colleague

Manager diverts her attention to other team members

Difficult team member is unresponsive and not participating in meeting

Colleague is distracted by the atmosphere generated by difficult team member

BEING ASSERTIVE

In order to remain calm, even when the difficult person confronting you may be angry and aggressive, you need to be assertive. Encouraging others to be aware of whether or not they are being assertive can help a difficult person move towards agreement.

29 Identify whether a difficult person is being aggressive, passive, or assertive.

30 Respect the rights of others and compromise when appropriate.

31 Listen to others if you want to be listened to yourself.

FACING AGGRESSION OR PASSIVITY

Aggression means being immovable on facts and being hard on people. A difficult person may react to criticism by being aggressive and obstructive, which can have a destructive effect on a team. Passivity means being soft on facts and being soft on people. A difficult passive person will not take action to resolve a situation and will make no effort to confront people. Although less likely to have acted hastily or upset others, a passive individual is more likely to have omitted to take action. This is often harder to find out about than an obvious mistake but can have a similar impact.

ENCOURAGING ASSERTIVENESS

When facing either aggression or passivity, you need to encourage the difficult person to be assertive while remaining assertive yourself. Assertiveness means being firm on facts and flexible with people. It is saying directly to others what you want, need, or feel. It is being honest with yourself and with others and recognizing that other people, including the difficult person, have the right to be heard and to have an opinion. Setting this example for your team will enable you to achieve better performance from difficult people.

POINTS TO REMEMBER

● The best way for your team to understand what assertive behaviour looks like is to observe you at work.

● Self-awareness and honest feedback should be encouraged so that team members are able to see assertiveness being demonstrated by others.

● Just as you have the right to be heard, it is important that the same respect should be shown to others.

USING DIFFERENT TYPES OF ASSERTIVE STATEMENTS

TYPE OF STATEMENT	EXAMPLES
FACTUAL A straightforward statement that gives facts, feedback, or information and makes clear your wishes, needs, wants, beliefs, opinions, or feelings.	● "As I see it, the system is working well." ● "I'd like you to be here by nine o'clock." ● "I feel very pleased with the way the situation has been resolved." ● "I liked the diagrams you included in your report."
EMPATHETIC A statement showing sensitivity that can be used to pre-empt an aggressive person, followed by an expression of your needs and wants.	● "I can see that the new procedure means extra work until you are used to it. However, I'd still like you to keep on working with it to give it a fair trial, please." ● "Although I know you're very busy at the moment, I need to ask you something, please."
DIVERGENT A statement that can establish whether there has been a misunderstanding between what was previously agreed, and what is actually happening.	● "As I recall, we agreed that Project X was top priority. You seem to be giving more time to Project Y. Can we please clarify which has top priority?" ● "We said we would hold meetings weekly. They seem to be fortnightly or monthly. We need to establish them regularly – every fortnight or every week as agreed."
EXPRESSIVE A statement expressing your negative feelings, letting other people know the adverse effect their behaviour is having on you, without becoming over-emotional.	● "When you're late back from lunch and the phones are busy, I feel annoyed you're not here to help. I'd like you to come back on time and take your turn on the phones." ● "I feel aggrieved when you ask my staff for answers. I'd like you to check with me first and if I can't provide answers, I'll direct you to the right person."
CONSEQUENT A statement that can be used as a warning when other people have failed to act, letting them know the consequences for them if they do not change their behaviour.	● "I'm not going to let any of my staff work on this project with your people, unless you give them access to the same training that your team was given." ● "This client's order is worth thousands. If we fail to respond to queries quickly enough and lose the account, it will have an adverse impact on the department."
RESPONSIVE A statement or question to find out the other person's views, needs, wants, or feelings, and to make sure that there is no misunderstanding between you.	● "What problems might that create?" ● "What would you prefer to do?" ● "I'd like to hear your views on this." ● "Which approach do you think is best?" ● "What are the plus and minus points from your point of view?"

23

CONFRONTING
DIFFICULT PEOPLE

Confronting difficult staff becomes necessary if avoidance has not worked. It then becomes an opportunity for change, but you need to think beforehand about how you are going to deal with the situation successfully and move people forward.

32 Check that difficult people understand the full impact of their behaviour.

33 Avoid prolonged eye contact in a confrontational situation.

CONFRONTING DIFFICULT PEOPLE

It is essential to remain calm, listen carefully, and be assertive. Empathize with the difficult person. Perhaps their anger is with themselves and not with you. Think about the words you are going to use. Aim for an 80/20 ratio, with you talking only 20 per cent of the time. Outline the situation as you see it and ask them if they can see the problem. If they cannot, then you will not be able to move on until you get them to see that there is a problem. Once you can agree on that, you can move on to agree actions to rectify or change the situation.

USING BODY LANGUAGE ▼
Body language is important when confronting difficult people. An open posture looks relaxed and friendly, whereas a closed posture can look unwelcoming.

Open arms, chin up, and desk at an angle to avoid creating a barrier

POSITIVE BODY LANGUAGE

Arm folded across chest, chin down, seeming unwilling to be interrupted

Cluttered desk gives the impression that the manager is too busy to talk

NEGATIVE BODY LANGUAGE

KEEPING SAFE

Confrontation may provoke emotional language or even physical aggression in a difficult person. It may also provoke an aggressive or uncharacteristic reaction in you. Think about how you are likely to react if the pressure builds, and plan what you are going to do. Be aware of your organization's disciplinary policy and recognize your role as its representative. Remain impartial and listen. Sometimes listening is all that is needed to help the person calm down and start thinking clearly. If you need to understand more, ask questions in a non-threatening tone. Make sure your body language and voice do not provoke further aggression.

MOVING PEOPLE FORWARD

When confronting difficult people, you are giving them feedback they may not want to hear. If they do not want to change, then they will bring up problems and barriers as excuses to prevent change. Listen to the problems and then plan how these can be overcome in future. Keep questioning until you have a clear agreed action plan. Then focus your questions on achieving the actions you have agreed between you so that you can move them forward.

DEALING WITH CONFRONTATION

Outline the situation as you see it

Listen carefully to other person's view of situation

Gain agreement that a problem exists

Use questioning to identify ways of rectifying the problem

Agree an action plan

Focus other person on achieving actions

FOCUSING ON ▶ THE FUTURE

By asking questions, John moved Susan forward from dwelling in the past to focusing on future opportunities. By agreeing actions that would make a difference, John succeeded in helping Susan to feel motivated and in control.

CASE STUDY

John, an engineer, had observed how Susan, his secretary, had recently become more difficult to motivate. At their next meeting, John asked whether there was a problem. Susan kept bringing up issues such as delays in IT training and upgrading her computer plus missed weekly meetings, all issues that had been resolved months ago. John felt aggrieved that Susan could not see how things had improved. He resolved to remain assertive and calmly to ask open questions to understand the problems from Susan's perspective. He asked Susan what was happening now and what she would like to see in future. They agreed an action plan to solve problems on ordering procedures and Susan took responsibility for the process. John followed up a week later and Susan confirmed that the new procedure was working well.

HELPING DIFFICULT PEOPLE THROUGH CHANGE

Helping people to accept that change provides opportunities is the starting point for reducing resistance to change. By anticipating it and planning ahead, you can manage it – rather than just reacting to the change and the responses of difficult people.

34 Make sure that you take the time to plan ahead for change.

35 Identify factors that help to drive change forwards.

36 Identify factors that restrain the pace of change.

IDENTIFYING REASONS FOR RESISTANCE

The most common reason for resistance to change is concern for self above other people. When you introduce change, consider the "What's In It For You?" (WIIFY) question to enable you to present the benefits of change that will overcome this attitude. Complete a forcefield analysis to see what will help and what will hinder change. Think what the difficult person's fears might be. If they have a low tolerance to change, emphasize what will remain unchanged while change is happening in other areas. They may misunderstand the purpose of change. The key to managing resistance is to communicate the benefits of the changes to come.

◀ **COMPLETING A FORCEFIELD ANALYSIS**
Create a table listing factors for change (driving forces) and those against it (restraining forces). Rate driving forces on a scale of plus 0-20, and restraining forces minus 0-20. Then add both scores to assess how likely a person is to accept the change. In this example, the change is the relocation of a key team member. Driving forces outnumber restraining forces, so the change should be accepted.

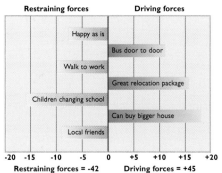

Restraining forces | Driving forces

Happy as is
Bus door to door
Walk to work
Great relocation package
Children changing school
Can buy bigger house
Local friends

-20 -15 -10 -5 0 +5 +10 +15 +20
Restraining forces = -42 | **Driving forces = +45**

WINNING SUPPORT FOR CHANGE

Enlisting the help of influential advocates of change can help you win over those who are opposed to it. In order to do this, you need to:

● List people who might be involved in, or affected by, change (known as stakeholders).

● Prioritize stakeholders according to how great an influence they have on others.

● Identify which stakeholders will support the change and which are likely to oppose it.

● Consider the likely objections of influential opposers, identify the benefits of change from their perspective, and start lobbying them.

● Involve influential supporters early so that they use their influence with others. Explain the advantages of the change clearly, and keep them abreast of progress so that they know what needs to be communicated.

MANAGING RESISTANCE

When planning change, consider how to clearly communicate your vision for the future. When people can visualize what change will look like when it is complete, they will be inspired to commit to it. Clear signs of improvement along the way to show that change is happening successfully need to be communicated. Conduct a stakeholder analysis to identify who will be your advocates for change. They will help you gain sufficient support to outweigh your critics. Understand that people's reactions to change tend to follow a recognized pattern and give them the time they need to move through the stages towards acceptance.

QUESTIONS TO ASK YOURSELF

Q Who is directly affected by this situation?

Q Who is in a position to influence others?

Q Who is likely to react badly or be displeased?

Q Have I prepared difficult people for change by involving them in planning for future scenarios?

REACTING ▶ TO CHANGE

In response to change, people tend to go through a series of emotional reactions. Shock and denial typically give way to a pining for the past and anger, which in turn leads to depression, and finally to acceptance. The duration of this process depends on the particular situation.

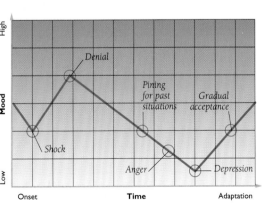

KNOWING WHEN TO STOP

If you cannot change a difficult person, you may have to change your attitude. It is sometimes better for the organization if you learn to live with, rather than continue to try to change, the individual. Alternatively, he or she may need to accept that it is time to leave.

37 Review a difficult person's overall performance to avoid hasty action.

38 Recognize when performance is standing still.

39 You may achieve results faster by changing your own behaviour.

ACCEPTING THE DIFFICULT PERSON

If the difficult person adds sufficient value to the organization, it may be that you will have to change your approach. Make an assessment to see if the person's strengths outweigh the weaknesses. Think about building on the strengths and putting in training or support to strengthen the weak areas. Ask yourself if you have looked objectively at that person's overall performance and taken full account of any achievements and contributions. Is it because he or she takes a different approach to your own and you find it difficult to handle? Accept that it can be extremely useful when problem-solving to have someone with a different perspective in the team.

◀ **CHANGING YOUR ATTITUDE**
Roy saw management meetings as a contest in which he was losing every round. This was affecting his self-confidence and his credibility with management colleagues. Using visualization, Roy changed his attitude to the meetings and his colleague. He was well-prepared each time and meetings became more productive.

CASE STUDY
Roy's colleague, Jane, was difficult and competitive. At management meetings, Jane frequently made suggestions as to how Roy's department could be improved. She would state her view aggressively, and Roy found it difficult to respond, although he could always think of an answer later. When he suggested that they meet regularly to discuss any problems between their two departments, Jane declined, saying she was too busy. Roy decided to change his attitude to Jane. Before meetings, Roy would visualize Jane criticizing his department on aspects he was working on improving. He visualized himself responding constructively to her comments and her more positive response. As a result, issues were resolved far more quickly and effectively during meetings, which was of benefit to the entire management team.

CHANGING YOUR OWN ATTITUDE

Empathizing with a difficult person can change your attitude to him or her. Place two chairs facing each other – one for you and one for the difficult person. Put a third chair at least 5 metres (16 feet) away, at a 90-degree angle to the other chairs. Sit opposite the difficult person's chair and state your point of view. Now sit in the other person's chair and state what you think is his or her point of view. Now stand on the third chair and look down on the two "people" facing each other. What new insights has this exercise given you into the difficult person's perspective? How will you change your approach in the light of this new information?

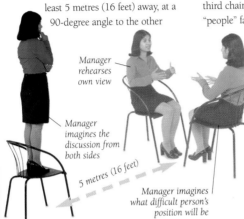

Manager rehearses own view

Manager imagines the discussion from both sides

5 metres (16 feet)

Manager imagines what difficult person's position will be

◀ **REVIEWING YOUR APPROACH**
Distancing yourself from the situation and looking at it from the other person's perspective can help you modify your approach accordingly. For example, you may realize that you are being overly emphatic, which can lead you to soften your approach.

REFUSING TO ACCEPT THE SITUATION

If a difficult person's behaviour is having a demoralizing effect on the team, you must manage the individual out of the situation. Look at the facts carefully. If this is the first time the person has gone beyond the limits you have set with the team, then ensure that your response is reasonable. If you have not been clear in communicating the limits, then you should now state them clearly to that person and specify how they can put the situation right. If the person cannot change in the time you specify, then you need to move them one step nearer to leaving the organization, according to normal disciplinary procedures.

40 Aim to improve performance – it is more cost-effective than dismissal.

41 Set realistic time scales for staff to demonstrate improvement.

WORKING FOR CO-OPERATION

A manager's primary aim is to gain the co-operation of difficult people. Plan your approach and use good communication skills in order to negotiate the best outcome for all parties.

PREPARING FOR CO-OPERATION

*K*nowing that you have planned and prepared carefully for a difficult meeting helps you feel more confident about it. Try initially for co-operation rather than conflict with a difficult person by aiming for a solution that benefits you both equally.

42 Note that a positive approach is sometimes all that is needed.

43 Plan to listen to objections before you respond by stressing benefits.

PLANNING FOR CO-OPERATION

A positive approach is often enough to win you co-operation from even the most difficult person. Prepare yourself to overcome objections to your proposals. Brainstorm what the objections might be, then think of the advantages of your proposals, including those that benefit the difficult person. Ask "If we could get round that, is there anything else that could stand in the way of this project?"

OVERCOMING OBJECTIONS

Exhaust all objections, then explain all the benefits

Ask difficult employee to rephrase any new objections

Offer further reassurance

Ask employee if he or she will support your proposals

If their answer is "No", ask why the suggestion is still not right

Outline further benefits and agree on future goals

SETTING GOALS FOR CO-OPERATION

Agreeing objectives with team members, customers, and other stakeholders reduces the risk of people becoming difficult because they failed to understand exactly what was asked of them. Goals should state what is expected in ways that mean something to people. Encourage people to write down goals in their own words so that they understand them clearly and will know when they have attained them. Set clear, well-defined objectives to ensure that people will not become difficult at a later stage because the goals set were unrealistic.

DOS AND DON'TS

✔ Do list all the benefits of what you are proposing before you have a discussion with a difficult person.

✔ Do make sure that some benefits answer the question "What's in it for me?" from the difficult person's point of view.

✘ Don't set objectives without agreeing deadlines and how they will be measured.

✘ Don't assume that you are both thinking the same thing – if you have any doubts, seek clarification by asking questions.

SETTING SMART OBJECTIVES

To help you set effective objectives, follow the SMART rule. This management acronym defines objectives as:
● Specific: they should clearly and unambiguously state requirements;
● Measurable: they must be quantifiable in terms of time, quality, quantity, and cost;
● Achievable: they should be within the

employee's capability, taking into account the resources available and authority levels;
● Relevant: they should be appropriate for the job/project and within the individual's control;
● Timely: they should have a realistic timescale for completion.

PREPARING FOR
DIFFICULT SITUATIONS

*Sometimes people are difficult when
a situation is stressful for them. Learn
how to prepare for interviews, inductions,
and appraisals so that you can offer
encouragement and reassurance to prevent
someone from becoming difficult.*

44 Ease nerves in
difficult situations
by asking easier
questions at first.

45 Greet a candidate
and accompany
them to the room.

46 Prepare by reading
an interviewee's
CV carefully.

INTERVIEWING PEOPLE

Concentrate on putting the candidate at ease,
since this will help them perform at their best. If
a candidate wants a job very much, he or she may
overreact by talking too much, or not enough,
or by becoming defensive at perceived "trick"
questions. Encourage the person to answer your
questions directly. If an interviewee strays off the
subject, bring them back to the point or explain
why you want a specific piece of information. If
the interviewee is reticent, rephrase some of your
questions or probe further on the point.

*Manager starts by
introducing herself
and explaining the
interview procedure*

◀ **BUILDING
RAPPORT**
*Use open body language and
smile encouragingly to help
put the interviewee at ease.
Avoid sitting on opposite
sides of a desk, as this will
create a barrier between you.*

*Interviewee has time
to relax and settle
into the interview*

CONDUCTING APPRAISALS

Give a potentially difficult team member time to prepare for the appraisal. Ensure that they know exactly what to expect, and prepare your questions thoroughly so that the appraisee does most of the talking. Illustrate your praise with examples of real achievements and focus your constructive criticism on areas that need development. Your appraisal should reflect a 2:1 ratio of positive feedback to constructive criticism. Create an action plan together to build on strengths and develop those areas that need improvement.

THINGS TO DO

1. Confirm the date and location of the appraisal at least two weeks in advance.

2. Provide the appraisee with guidance and the means to self-assess.

3. Read through current job description and last year's appraisal and action plan.

4. Note down training undertaken, project results, and any other achievements.

5. Plan the sequence of the appraisal.

6. Prepare questions to ask.

Appraisee notes actions arising from discussion

◀ **APPRAISING EFFECTIVELY**
Use the appraisal to focus staff on the future, identifying development needs and aspirations, giving direction, and agreeing expected contribution.

POINTS TO REMEMBER

● Preparation is the key to dealing with difficult situations effectively.

● Making checklists of the preparation needed for interviews, appraisals, and induction saves you time in the long run.

● Putting yourself in the other person's situation will help you to anticipate difficulties.

● An effective manager follows up on all the actions agreed.

INDUCTING NEW RECRUITS

An induction can be stressful for a new employee who does not understand the culture of a new organization. Yet new recruits can often provide fresh and invaluable perspectives on your way of working. Value a new employee's honest opinion rather than seeing them as difficult and unlikely to "fit in". Their feedback can help you develop your team and make induction more effective. Think who could act as a mentor to the newcomer. If there is someone who also views questioning as a learning process, the benefits will be two-way.

MANAGING FOR CO-OPERATION

People may become difficult if they feel that they are being poorly managed or are working without clear direction. Develop your own management skills and learn to adapt your leadership style in order to win co-operation from difficult individuals.

47 Develop an open culture in which staff give each other feedback.

48 Recognize that new staff may need more support.

49 Encourage initiative in experienced team members.

MANAGING EFFECTIVELY

Effective management involves carrying out tasks successfully by deploying resources efficiently to achieve the results required. Check that you have defined roles and objectives clearly, planned and organized resources according to your priorities, and agreed the controls you will use. If someone is still being difficult, you may not have involved that person sufficiently at the planning stage. To keep the individual on board with the rest of the team, make sure that you carry out reviews of progress together.

MANAGING PROJECTS

Ensure that everyone involved understands at the outset the project's objectives and constraints, its key milestones, who is responsible for what, and who will be involved at which stages. By doing this, you avoid the risk of team members becoming difficult later as a result of not being given all the information they need. Reviews, planned in advance and held frequently throughout the project, can then help you to maintain the balance between quality and performance within budget and to the agreed timescale.

QUESTIONS TO ASK YOURSELF

Q Do I consistently set fair objectives for team members?

Q Do I monitor each individual's overall performance?

Q Have I anticipated and removed any barriers to achieving objectives?

Q Are there any recurring problems that indicate a need for me to develop my skills?

50 Delegate to show trust in people – this can help to prevent them from becoming difficult.

LEADING PEOPLE

Be prepared to adapt your leadership style with someone you find difficult, because the style you find comfortable will not work in all situations. Avoid telling someone how to do things – instead say what needs to be achieved and why, letting him or her work out how to reach the goal. A leader must also delegate well or risk overload or stress that affects the team, who may react by becoming difficult. Brief delegates on the outcomes and standards required, giving them the authority needed, and agreeing when you will review progress.

PROVIDING FEEDBACK

Feedback helps people to see themselves as others see them. Without feedback, a team member may continue to perform in a way that is no longer effective. However, feedback can be seen as a threat. Someone who expects negative criticism may become withdrawn or defensive. Give feedback regularly until it becomes accepted as the usual routine. Focus your feedback on behaviour or results rather than the person, and on what is important and within his or her control to change.

51 Give constructive feedback in order to encourage staff.

▼ COMPARING FEEDBACK
Feedback can have a positive effect or a negative one. Positive feedback is constructive and concentrates on what is important. Negative feedback is judgmental, overcritical, or irrelevant.

POSITIVE FEEDBACK

NEGATIVE FEEDBACK

Is given as soon after the event as possible

Is delivered one to one

Is constructive, factual, and specific

Is balanced and of future benefit to the recipient

Overwhelms the recipient with too much information

Is delivered in front of other people

Is overly judgmental, critical, or tainted with emotion

Dwells too much on the past

HANDLING POOR PERFORMANCE

*E*mployees who are under too much or too little stress may under-perform. Spot the signs early so that you can help a difficult person operate at constructive stress levels. If performance fails to improve, you may have to dismiss the difficult individual.

52 See that people develop through overcoming challenges.

53 Watch for changes in someone's behaviour.

54 Set an objective to stretch a difficult person and observe what happens.

IDENTIFYING STRESS

Everyone needs a certain amount of stress to fuel performance and experience the personal satisfaction that comes with overcoming challenges. If a difficult person seems lethargic, bored, and has no enthusiasm for the job, then he or she is not being challenged enough. Alternatively, if the person appears angry and seems to be sabotaging his or her own performance, then these could be signs of too much stress. Whatever the problem, you need to review the team member's role with them and set clear objectives. Discuss all possible courses of action that can be taken. For example, if the individual is under too much stress, it may be possible to delegate aspects of their role to someone else.

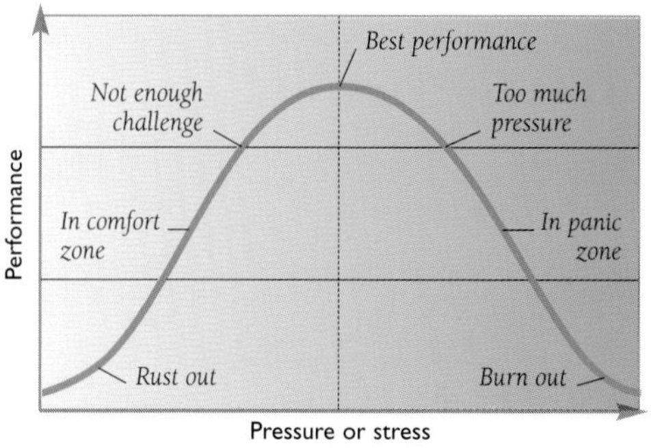

Best performance

Not enough challenge

Too much pressure

In comfort zone

In panic zone

Performance

Rust out

Burn out

Pressure or stress

◄ **UNDERSTANDING THE STRESS CURVE**
This diagram shows how performance is affected as stress levels change. A lack of stress at one end of the curve, and a serious overload of stress at the opposite end have the same effect: performance deteriorates drastically.

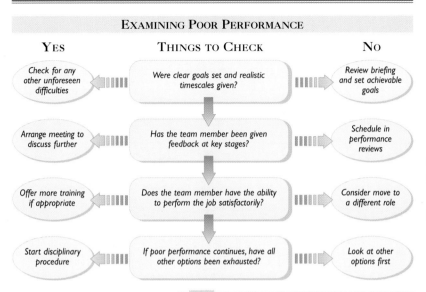

EXAMINING POOR PERFORMANCE

YES	THINGS TO CHECK	NO
Check for any other unforeseen difficulties	Were clear goals set and realistic timescales given?	Review briefing and set achievable goals
Arrange meeting to discuss further	Has the team member been given feedback at key stages?	Schedule in performance reviews
Offer more training if appropriate	Does the team member have the ability to perform the job satisfactorily?	Consider move to a different role
Start disciplinary procedure	If poor performance continues, have all other options been exhausted?	Look at other options first

DEALING WITH POOR ▲ PERFORMANCE

When you are dealing with poor performance, make sure that the person knows exactly what is expected and has every opportunity to rectify the situation.

55 Before dismissing someone, check that you have offered all reasonable support and encouragement.

DISMISSING PEOPLE

If all your attempts to help the difficult person to perform well fail, then he or she will have to leave. If the problem is lack of ability, then try to move the person to a more suitable position within the organization. If the problem is persistent difficult behaviour or poor performance, then you need to follow your organization's disciplinary procedure and give the person notice of dismissal. This is always written, but also needs to be delivered face to face. Prepare what you will say carefully, because the reasons you give for dismissal may be quoted in any unfair dismissal claim.

POINTS TO REMEMBER

- Emotional rejection of the job and the organization should be confronted as soon as it becomes apparent in an individual.
- The organization's role in creating the problem should also be taken into account.
- Make sure that you read up on your organization's disciplinary procedure and guidance notes.
- In some cases a professional career counsellor may be needed.

BEING OBJECTIVE

When dealing with difficult people, it helps to stay objective. Being objective demands a high level of self-awareness. Knowing your own biases and personality helps you understand what stands in the way of your working effectively with other people.

56 Avoid allowing your judgment to be clouded by a single issue.

57 Be aware that everyone listens selectively.

58 Respond to the person in front of you, not someone they remind you of.

RECOGNIZING YOUR OWN BIAS

Your background, your education and training, past experiences at work or school, childhood influences, parents or friends, and groups to which you belong all play a part in shaping your view of the world. Recognizing that we all look at the world through our own filters helps you to empathize with a person who, at first, appears difficult. Unconsciously, you may both be finding that the differences between you are forming a barrier to effective communication and to viewing issues objectively.

MAKING ASSUMPTIONS

By being aware that your viewpoint may be biased, you are less likely to make assumptions about people based on your subjective opinion alone. To avoid making wrong assumptions, keep an open mind and listen to the views of others. Take notes and summarize to ensure that, in any conversation with a difficult person, you both leave with the same understanding. Avoid forming an opinion first and then choosing the facts to support it. Instead, question to clarify and gather facts, then use these facts to make your decision. Base your decisions on behaviour and performance, not on personality or background.

CULTURAL DIFFERENCES

People from different cultures may perceive each other differently. Americans and some Europeans, for example, often greet newcomers as if they were old friends, which can appear insincere or disrespectful to people from more reserved cultures, such as in Asia and the Middle East.

OVERCOMING DIFFERENT TYPES OF BIAS

TYPE OF BIAS	HOW TO OVERCOME IT
HALO/HORNS Allowing one or two favourable or unfavourable qualities to influence your judgment of the whole person.	● Make sure that you have established the facts on the individual's performance. ● Assess how important the problem is in the light of the team member's total performance.
"SIMILAR TO ME" A tendency to favour – even recruit and promote – people you see as being similar to yourself.	● Identify the individual's strengths. ● Look at development areas for the individual. ● Determine what skills or experience are needed for the job or project.
PREJUDICE Letting background or culture cloud your judgment about people or a person who reminds you of someone.	● Ask yourself who the individual reminds you of. ● Identify what it is specifically about their behaviour or performance that is the problem. ● Assess what preconceptions you might have.
DISTORTED CONCEPTS Making assumptions based on misuse of psychology, such as assuming that all salespeople have to be extrovert.	● Identify the requirements of the job. ● Decide how much experience and which qualifications or skills are really needed. ● Ask yourself what your assumptions are based on.
STEREOTYPING Having a mental image of the ideal worker, then assessing people against this rather than on actual strengths.	● Look at what must be achieved in the job or project. ● Check that the objectives you have in mind are realistic. ● Identify the essential/desirable characteristics that will enable an individual to do the job.

EVALUATING INFORMATION

Knowing that you may have your own stereotypes about good workers, and that you can give too much weight to your similarities with people who appear to have much in common with you, helps you to evaluate difficult people more objectively. It is important to assess the difficult person and his or her behaviour overall. Make sure you are not just remembering the most recent example of difficult behaviour and overlooking previous co-operation and achievements. Ask yourself whether you did anything, perhaps unintentionally, that may have led to this change in behaviour.

59 Make sure that you avoid jumping to conclusions too quickly.

60 Ask questions and listen actively to avoid making wrong assumptions.

QUESTIONING AND LISTENING

Asking the right questions, at the right time, will speed communication by getting the response you need quickly and effectively. The key skill is listening to the response and looking for clues as to what your next question should be.

61 Be aware that silence has the same effect as a probing question.

62 Prepare questions in advance and listen for clues as to what your next question should be.

USING OPEN QUESTIONS

The best way to find out why an individual is being difficult is to ask them diplomatically. Use open questions to encourage a difficult person to open up and reveal what is causing the difficulties (work-related or personal). By using open questions you avoid leading someone into stating what you assume is the problem and encourage them into thinking through a reply. The opposite of an open question is a closed one, such as "Did you…?", which elicits only the answer "Yes" or "No".

ASKING OPEN QUESTIONS

There are many ways of phrasing an open question. Try asking questions that start with words such as "What ..?", "Who...?", "When...?", and "How...?", which demand a more detailed response. Here are a few examples.

❝ *What do you think is the cause of the current situation?* ❞

❝ *What do you think would be a better way?* ❞

❝ *When could that be done?* ❞

❝ *Who else could we bring in to help with this?* ❞

❝ *How can we resolve this problem quickly?* ❞

❝ *What are your ideas on this?* ❞

ALLOWING TIME TO RESPOND

Open questions give the difficult person time to think and form a response. If you suspect that the individual has not thought an issue through, then you can ask a question to help them weigh up the pros and cons of proposed actions, such as "What are the advantages and disadvantages of…?" or "What benefits and pitfalls do you foresee if…?". If you need time to consider the team member's response, say something like, "That's an interesting point, I'd like to take time to think about that." A pause gives you time to reflect, and the other person may fill the silence with the very information you wanted.

63 Use pauses often to give you both time to think.

Manager asks for a minute to consider the points raised

Team member demands an opinion on a sensitive issue

STAYING IN CONTROL ▶
When a difficult team member attempts to badger a response from you, avoid answering before you are ready. Pausing to consider what has been said shows that you are taking their views seriously.

64 Avoid asking "Why?" too often; it can be stressful.

65 Remember not only to listen but to show that you are listening.

LISTENING ACTIVELY

Encourage a difficult person to keep talking, without having to agree or disagree with what is being said, by employing non-committal words in a positive tone of voice. For example, you can use "Uh huh…", "Ah…", and "Please tell me more…" as prompts. Think of something to say that links to what has been said earlier, using the individual's own words, to show that you are listening actively, for example, "You said earlier that you found that challenging. In what way…?" Paraphrase, summarize, and restate the other person's comments in your own words to demonstrate active listening.

USING LISTENING SKILLS

TYPE OF LISTENING	USING METHOD EFFECTIVELY
MIRRORING Using the same words as a difficult person to elicit information and help your understanding.	Imagine yourself in the other person's position, and show understanding by talking little and encouraging with nods and words.
EXPLORING Noticing words given extra emphasis or unusual words that indicate strong feelings.	Use open questions to discover the reasons behind a person's statements. Observe body language as well as voice.
AFFIRMING Reflecting ideas and feelings expressed by the person and summarizing the facts agreed.	Check for the difficult person's agreement and build on their suggestions to guide the conversation towards the desired result.

LISTENING TO VOICE AS WELL AS WORDS

If you wish to establish a real rapport with the difficult team member, you need to listen to the pace at which he or she is speaking and mirror that pace. If the individual is speaking thoughtfully and slowly, then a quick, staccato question from you will sound like gunfire and will cut them short, rather than encouraging openness so that you can understand why they are being difficult. Listen to the pitch and tone of the voice. If someone is very nervous or uptight, then their pitch will tend to be higher and more strained. If their tone is shaky and uncertain, then the team member might be indicating doubts.

66 Listen for defensive strategies being used to deflect you.

▼ REACTING TO PACE AND PITCH

Judge how an individual is feeling according to the pace and tone of their voice, and use the same pace and tone yourself to build rapport.

Manager listens patiently to slow speech and plans a calm, reasoned response

67 Notice repeated or unusual words that indicate areas to probe.

POINTS TO REMEMBER

● A manager who listens to his or her team encourages individuals to perform at their best.

● Criticizing ideas without consideration should be avoided if you are to encourage people to contribute suggestions.

● Many constructive discussions are destroyed by failing to focus on what is important.

● Maintaining eye contact, looking enthusiastic and seeking to learn from the conversation helps aid concentration while listening.

IDENTIFYING HIDDEN AGENDA

Once you have asked the right questions, listen to what is being said and pay special attention to repeated words or phrases that indicate what is really bothering the difficult person. If he or she is repeating words or phrases like "too difficult…", "daunting…", and "not my fault…", these indicate a lack of confidence in their ability to achieve the task in hand. Stressing words such as "important to me…", "challenging…", and "vital…", indicates that these are key issues for the individual. Listen, too, to what is not being said, because this can give you similarly important clues as to which questions to ask to find out whether or not the team member has a hidden agenda.

68 Note that emphasized words indicate what is really important to the individual.

FOLLOWING THE FIVE POINTS

Check that you are responding to a difficult person in the most constructive way by running through the following Five Points or Five Ps in your mind as you are speaking:

● Pace: am I speaking too slowly or too quickly? Do I seem unsure or hesitant?

● Projection: is my voice raised or is it mumbling or quiet? Do I need to speak more loudly/quietly?

● Pause: how many pauses for thought are there? Am I talking at the individual or taking time to consider?

● Pitch: does my voice sound strained? Is it higher, tighter, or more nervous than normal?

● Pronunciation: am I enunciating properly and speaking each word clearly?

HEARING ▶ YOURSELF
Listen to your voice to ensure that you are being clear and conveying the right message.

COMMUNICATING NON-VERBALLY

A difficult person will understand your approach through non-verbal communication long before you speak. Being able to observe the other person's non-verbal signs, to know when a person is about to become difficult, puts you one step ahead.

69 Be responsive whether you like or agree with people or not.

70 Notice non-verbal warnings of the response to come.

71 Build rapport with a difficult person by using mirroring.

PROJECTING THE RIGHT MESSAGE

You can use Neuro Linguistic Programming (NLP) to increase your rapport with a difficult person. Research indicates that communication is 55 per cent understood through body language, 38 per cent through tone of voice, and only 7 per cent through actual words themselves. NLP provides some useful techniques for successful non-verbal communication. Act in a confident manner and you will start to feel confident. You can also use NLP to build rapport and trust with another person. By adopting an alert but relaxed posture yourself, you encourage a difficult individual to mirror your positive body language, which can help them to participate more fully.

Manager leans forwards slightly, appearing alert, relaxed, and ready to listen

◀ **PROJECTING THE RIGHT MESSAGE**
To demonstrate that you are interested in what the other person is about to say, make eye contact and sit well back in your chair, with no crossed legs or arms, leaning forwards about five degrees from vertical.

INTERPRETING EYE MOVEMENTS

CONSTRUCTING IMAGES
A person looking up and to their right is usually using their imagination or picturing something in their mind.

REMEMBERING SOUNDS
Someone looking to their left is usually remembering a sound or recalling something that has been said in the past.

REMEMBERING IMAGES
Someone looking up to their left is often summoning to mind a remembered image from the past.

INTERNAL DIALOGUE
A person looking down to their left is likely to be hearing an inner voice as he talks to himself inside his head.

CONSTRUCTING SOUNDS
A person looking to their right is likely to be concentrating on forming a verbal response in their mind.

HAVING FEELINGS
Someone looking down to their right is in touch with their emotions, and is checking how they feel about something.

72 Note that eye movements show you how to build rapport.

POINTS TO REMEMBER

● Listening for visual, auditory, and kinaesthetic words or phrases enables you to adapt to the cues.

● Folded arms indicate that you are touching on a sensitive issue.

● Responding with similar sensory words to those being used by a difficult person builds rapport.

USING THE SENSES TO INTERPRET INFORMATION

When people think and communicate, they tend to use three main senses: visual (seeing), auditory (hearing), and kinaesthetic (feeling). If you observe the eye positions and speech of a talking person, you can guess that person's way of processing information and use it to build rapport. For example, if someone is looking upwards and using visual words such as, "I don't see what you mean", respond with similar language such as, "Let's look at it this way …". If a person is expressing themselves in an auditory way, such as by saying "I don't like the sound of this", respond with a phrase such as "Let's talk it through …". If someone says, "This doesn't feel right", try phrases such as, "Let's take care of any concerns you may have …".

EXPLORING SOLUTIONS

Searching for solutions needs skilful questioning and an innovative approach. You need to be able to find solutions that even the most difficult person will want to put into action. Exploring ideas together will help you to achieve this.

73 Ask questions to understand the other person's needs and ideas.

74 Look for points of agreement to keep the discussion constructive.

ENCOURAGING OPEN DIALOGUE

You can encourage two-way dialogue and openness with the difficult person by signalling what you are going to say next. Use phrases such as "Can I suggest…" and "I would like to ask…". If you disagree about some things, do not emphasize them. Instead summarize the points you can agree on to underline a positive approach. If you do have to disagree, give your reasons first.

SPOTTING INFLUENCING STYLES

COERCIVE
This style involves using a more compelling, authoritative approach, even coercion, in order to gain results.

PARTICIPATORY
Influencing by participation requires an encouraging, sharing approach that inspires trust and confidence.

PERSUASIVE
People using the persuasive style of influencing will use logic and emotion in order to achieve their objectives.

INFLUENCING DISCUSSIONS

Influencing means being able to understand another person's needs and matching them with a corresponding benefit of doing what you propose. Influencing can be subtle, for example you can influence by using the word "suggest" instead of "propose", or it can involve sophisticated questioning to explore needs and find out what motivates the other person. Most people have a preferred style of influencing, and might view a person with a different style as being difficult.

SEEKING COMMITMENT

You will be able to tell from an individual's body language and tone of voice which possible solutions he or she favours. Ask the person to summarize the key actions that you have agreed. If the team member has not really agreed to some of these solutions, he or she will change their wording or miss them out altogether. If they appear enthusiastic and start to add detail to the plan you have agreed, you have gained the team member's commitment.

75 Encourage the person to use active verbs for actions, such as "save", instead of vague words like "liaise".

ENSURING ACTION

Ask questions such as, "What needs to be done, how well, by when, and by whom?" The action plan that results should identify the goal, the activities (mainly the other person's) that are needed, the resources (including who else might be involved), milestones on the way, a realistic timetable, and the outcome expected.

GAINING COMMITMENT

Establish purpose of meeting: to explore solutions together

Agree agenda of items for discussion

Open two-way dialogue

Agree action plan

Ask team member to summarize agreed actions

▼ PRODUCING AN ACTION PLAN
Always draw up an action plan to provide a record of actions you have agreed. It can be simple or detailed, but it should state clearly who should be doing what and by when.

ACTION PLAN

No	Key Actions	Who	When
1	Draw up a graph showing the sales results over the last three quarters	CM	End April
2	Look at the sales strategy and identify potential areas for growth	LT	End June
3	Generate 350 new sales leads per month	SL	End July
4	Commission new corporate logo in line with brand values	CM	End Sep

Date agreed for completion of action

Initials of person responsible for the action

Detailed description of action planned, including any measures agreed

NEGOTIATING SOLUTIONS

Finding and negotiating the right solutions demands creativity and flexibility. You need to look for solutions that will work for the difficult person and represent a winning situation for you and your team. The key is to find out first what the difficult person wants.

> **76** Explain why you are asking questions to allay suspicion about your motives.

QUESTIONS TO ASK YOURSELF

Q Have I shown and encouraged flexibility and creativity in suggesting solutions?

Q Can I hold my ground in the face of tough opposition?

Q Have I taken notes of the key points agreed?

Q Am I conceding something that will create an awkward precedent with other people?

Q Do I review every negotiation to identify how to improve?

FOCUSING ON HIGHER GOALS

If you cannot get a difficult person to agree to an objective, use questions to elicit a higher goal on which both of you can agree. For example, if you want to expand the team and your colleague wants to keep the team as it is, you need to move on from this stalemate with a goal that satisfies both of you, such as increasing the team's output. You can then ask questions to explore what benefits the other person would like, and other possibilities may arise from this discussion.

▼ GAINING AGREEMENT

In order to move from stalemate to a situation of mutual co-operation, you need to ask lots of questions and seek out a higher goal on which you can both agree.

Team member refuses to agree to objective

Seek out a higher goal on which you can both agree

Establish good rapport while agreeing new goal

Ask what benefits the other person would like

Manager asks more questions

Both parties agree on a new goal

NEGOTIATING THE BEST SOLUTION

When exploring solutions, many people view the negotiation as a tug of war with four outcomes. In fact, the only outcome you should aim for is the win-win scenario or one in which, rather than trying to take a bigger slice of cake from the other person, you look instead at how you can make the cake bigger for both of you. Ask questions that will expand the options for you both by generating other possibilities. Only when you have generated and explored a variety of possibilities together should you move towards making a decision. Explore areas of agreement to identify a solution to which you can both commit. A difficult person is more likely to agree to your proposal after you have explored all the options together.

POINTS TO REMEMBER

● To negotiate a mutually beneficial solution, open questions should be used to find out what the other person hopes to achieve.

● A manager who is willing to challenge past practice makes a good negotiator.

Manager is fair and assertive

Manager is too passive

▲ I WIN/YOU WIN
The ideal outcome is achieved by acknowledging the rights of both parties and searching for ways in which both can win.

▲ I LOSE/YOU WIN
An unsatisfactory solution is reached by passive manager who admits defeat, allowing the other person to "win".

77 Identify where you disagree while negotiating to avoid trouble later.

Manager is too aggressive

Manager is too combative

78 Summarize to clarify that you both have the same understanding.

▲ I WIN/YOU LOSE
Complete disregard is shown for the other person by a manipulative manager who seeks to win at their expense.

▲ I LOSE/YOU LOSE
Both parties lose out because a manager seeks to avoid or obstruct negotiation rather than let the other person win.

AGREEING THE SOLUTION

*I*n order to achieve long-term success
with a difficult person, he or she needs to
accept ownership of an action plan. There
also needs to be continued co-operation
throughout the life of the project, or until
all the action plan points are completed.

79 Ask an individual
to summarize their
action plan to help
them commit to it.

▲ **OBSERVING BEHAVIOUR**
*A person who has accepted ownership of a
project or plan will be enthusiastic, keen
to put ideas into practice, and happy to
discuss their work with colleagues.*

ASSESSING OWNERSHIP

Observing behaviour will help you assess
whether the difficult person has accepted
ownership of the plan and is committed to it.
As the individual summarizes and notes down
the actions you have both agreed, note the
language and tone of voice used. Are they looking
forward to completing the actions and sounding
enthusiastic about the solution agreed? Explore
any reluctance or uncertainty and ask the person
to summarize any further actions you both agree
may be needed as a result. Having noted all the
action points, together with any support you
agreed to give, the team member should copy the
action plan to you for your next review together.

IMPLEMENTING AN AGREEMENT

Check that the difficult person is clear about his or
her responsibilities. Using the BOB CARD checklist,
review the background, including any sensitivities
or history to the project. Assess what will or will not
be included, analyze the constraints that limit what
can be achieved, review your assumptions, such as
the availability of help from others, agree reporting
requirements (setting review dates), and specify the
deliverables. The plan needs to be comprehensive
but also easy to understand and use.

THINGS TO DO

1. Ask the other person to
suggest a realistic timescale
for reviewing progress on
agreed actions.

2. Check that actions agreed
at the last review have
been completed.

3. Praise your team member
for what has been achieved.

USING THE **BOB CARD** CHECKLIST

The BOB CARD is a useful management tool that can help you to transform an agreement into an implementation plan.

● **Background:** review how this point was reached.

● **Objectives:** what is needed in terms of quantity, quality, time, and cost.

● **Boundaries:** the scope of the job or project – what will be included or excluded and authority levels.

● **Constraints:** usually resources such as time, people, or cost.

● **Assumptions:** check that the plan is based on realistic assumptions – if guesses are wrong, change the plan.

● **Reporting:** decide at the planning stage how to control and report on the work.

● **Deliverables:** describe what will be delivered by each phase and on final completion of the project.

CHECKING THE SOLUTION IS SAFE

Agree a solution that is Suitable, Acceptable, Feasible, and Enduring (SAFE). An agreement is suitable if it fits the current situation and the timing is right. How acceptable will it be to the rest of the team or any other stakeholders? What resources and budget will be needed to see it through? Given the time and resource constraints, how practical or feasible is this idea? How long will it take before the perceived benefits are realized? This could have an impact on how enduring the agreement will be. When you have satisfactory answers to each of these questions, you will know that the proposed agreement is SAFE.

▼ CHECKING TIMING

Look at timing in advance to highlight any potential pitfalls at the earliest opportunity, enabling changes to be made that turn the agreement into a realistic implementation plan.

Manager checks overlap of project priorities with team member

80 Identify activities, resources, roles, and deadlines in your plan.

DEALING WITH CONFLICT

When faced with a difficult person who refuses to perform, it is important to have coping strategies in place. Learn how to work through conflict successfully.

MANAGING YOUR OWN RESPONSES

When coping with a difficult person, a manager may need to contribute much more than 50 per cent to the communication process. Only by being highly self-aware and in control of your own responses will you be able to manage those of the difficult person.

> **81** Be aware of your own responses and their effect on the other person.

POINTS TO REMEMBER

- Your own body language should be checked to ensure that it is not provoking a difficult situation.
- If a difficult person has tensed any muscles, this should be observed and mirrored.
- Eye contact should be maintained and words, tone, and pace of voice should be matched.

STAYING IN RAPPORT

When you do not immediately understand what is going on because a person is sending out confused signals or seems resistant or hostile, staying in rapport is vital. Maintain eye contact and mirror the person's body language. Try to speak at the same pace and in the same tone and volume, and match your breathing. Use the same language. As rapport grows, you will feel more empathy until you can begin to predict how the person will respond.

THINKING AHEAD

To gain a better understanding of the points of view of the situation, first move into deeper rapport to empathize better with the difficult person; second, check your own point of view; and third, mentally distance yourself to observe the two of you occasionally. As you move from observing back to empathy, what new insights do you have on the situation? What advice can you give yourself now for handling the difficult person more effectively? Decide on the options you think will be most useful to you and try one on the difficult person. Observe the response. If the option did not work well, revisit the three points of view and try other options until you get a positive response.

▼ **DISTANCING YOURSELF**
Take a step back from the conversation to examine your own point of view, then imagine that you are observing the situation from a distance. This gives you space to decide what to do next.

Manager deepens rapport to empathize more

Manager mentally distances himself still further in order to observe

Manager takes a mental step back to check his own point of view

---

82 Check rapport by changing posture and observing if it is mirrored.

83 Empathize with the other person to maintain rapport.

DOS AND DON'TS

✔ Do describe outcomes you want in a positive way, for example, "Continue doing ..."

✔ Do be aware that your own gestures can signal tension or distract from your message.

✔ Do persevere – coping with conflict requires patience and persistence.

✘ Don't be negative when describing outcomes you want, for example, "Don't stop..."

✘ Don't stare but note that people who avoid eye contact may have something to hide.

✘ Don't put your hand over your mouth – it looks as though you are hiding something.

TAKING THE HEAT OUT OF THE SITUATION

When a difficult person is behaving aggressively, you need to know how to take the immediate heat out of the situation. Only when you have calmed the person down will you be able to regain his or her attention and move forward into productive discussion.

84 Avoid interrupting or prejudging; just listen and evaluate what is being said.

85 Take time to analyze the facts of a situation.

▼ DRAWING UP A PROBLEM TABLE
Create a problem table to enable you and the difficult person to identify the difficulties involved and work on devising a solution.

CREATING A DIVERSION

Asking a question that requires thought to answer is the simplest diversion of all. Ask the person to write down the advantages and disadvantages of what he or she proposes. Immediately, the person will look at the problem one step removed from both of you. If he or she needs further time to calm down, work through a problem table together. By gathering facts, the focus moves from the issues between you to actions that need to be taken.

PROBLEM TABLE

Analysis	Scale of problem	Current situation	Ideal situation	Action
Consolidated group report is never completed in time for monthly board meeting	A total of 12 divisional reports containing month-end figures need collating and summarizing by 5th of the following month to form group report	Fastest consolidation was by 10th of following month. Board is growing increasingly impatient	Board receive the consolidated group report to read 5 days before their board meeting takes place on 10th of the month	Cut-off date for monthly management accounts to be moved forwards to 25th of month to enable earlier production of month-end figures for divisional reports
Describe problem as fully as possible	*Detail size, duration, timescale, frequency, etc.*	*Outline the situation as it stands now*	*Describe what you want to see happen*	*Record actions agreed to rectify the problem*

Team member
becomes less
hostile as he
assesses facts

Manager guides
team member
through completing
problem table

LEADING THE DIFFICULT PERSON

To lead the difficult person, use mirroring and empathize with his or her current state. Decide on the behaviour that you wish to cultivate in the person and gently change aspects of your own body language to encourage it. Check whether the person's body language and words are consistent. If the individual mirrors you, then you have established rapport and can move the person away from a negative attitude by adopting body language that indicates a positive state.

▲ WORKING THROUGH A PROBLEM TABLE
Filling in a problem table with a difficult individual encourages you both to look at the facts of a problem rather than emotive issues surrounding it. It also promotes co-operation and collaboration.

86 Avoid cutting someone short by saying "Yes, but..."

POINTS TO REMEMBER

● Discussion of a problem should happen at the right time and in the right place.

● Time out may need to be taken if either party becomes heated and needs to cool down.

● A person's body language should be matched until they are ready to follow your lead.

● If there are options you can live with, the other person should be allowed to choose from these.

LEAVING AN ESCAPE ROUTE

It is important to avoid cornering a difficult individual and leaving them no way out other than to fight past you. Unless you leave them an escape route, you risk jeopardizing your finding a solution together. Allow the difficult person the freedom to set his or her own goals and timescales within a broad framework you both agree. Always leave at least two options so that the person still has an element of choice as to which way to go and therefore a way of saving "face".

AGREEING GROUND RULES

*S*tarting with an agreement on ground rules for working together is often easier to achieve than agreeing on the solution to the problem between you, and is a positive first step towards working more effectively with difficult people.

87 Use ground rules to set boundaries for one person or all team members.

88 Always set a time limit for discussions.

DEFINING GROUND RULES

Ground rules are guidelines or limits within which you agree to work. The first rule that focuses two individuals on coming to a solution is to set a time limit for the discussion. Other useful rules include listening to each other, looking at the benefits of other people's proposals rather than for reasons why they will not work, maintaining confidentiality, not interrupting each other, and taking turns to speak. Agreeing the ground rules at the beginning of a meeting can put a check on everyone's behaviour.

ESTABLISHING RULES▼
Ground rules help you to deal with any number of difficult people within the team. If people are to explore solutions together, everyone must abide by the rules or the meeting will lose its positive momentum.

Difficult team member reacts defensively to colleague's interruption

Manager reiterates rule that everyone must listen to each other

Difficult team member interrupts colleague with criticism

At World Trading
we are committed to:

1

Answering your telephone call
courteously within 3 rings

2

Responding immediately to any
complaints by telephone and in
writing within 24 hours

3

Ensuring a high level of expertise in
our Customer Service Advisers
through a programme of continuous
training and development

A. Smith

A. Smith
Managing Director

DEVELOPING A CHARTER

A person can be difficult if he or she does not understand how to interact with others in different situations. If someone deals with customers, for example, he or she must know what you promise your customers so that they understand customers' expectations and the part they have to play in their delivery. Draw up a customer charter setting out the level of service that the customer can expect. If the person is being difficult about doing the same as the rest of the team, a guideline on what you expect from team members will help.

◀ SETTING CUSTOMER CARE STANDARDS
Ensure that staff know the level of service they are expected to provide by drawing up a customer charter. The charter should state what your organization is prepared to do to guarantee customer satisfaction and quality care.

WRITING A SERVICE LEVEL AGREEMENT

If whole teams or departments view each other as difficult people, then a service level agreement between teams or departments may be needed. This outlines the service standards or performance levels that each department or team can expect from the other. Service level agreements minimize areas of potential difficulty because the levels of performance that each party can expect are laid down. The agreement can also contain penalties for non-compliance. Enter into such an agreement positively, recognizing that the benefit of an agreement that has been well thought through is that it will clarify for everyone exactly what it is important to achieve and maintain. Having a clear statement of service levels also makes the review process simpler and variations can more quickly be brought back on track.

89 Check that everyone knows what the service standards are.

POINTS TO REMEMBER

● Writing ground rules on a flipchart ensures that everyone is able to see and agree them.

● Charters or service level agreements clearly set out the standards expected.

● Being clear about what you expect from the outset reduces potential for conflict.

WORKING THROUGH CONFLICT

View conflict as a chance to understand the needs of the difficult person and how to influence that person to achieve the result you need. By facing up to conflict and acknowledging there is a problem, you have an opportunity to solve the problem together.

90 Describe behaviour that is causing problems and the effect it is having.

FACING THE CONFLICT

It is important to deal with the behaviour you are confronted with at that moment. Behaviour is not constant, it stops and starts, improves and grows worse, so you need to adjust your response in a measured way. Face conflict openly by giving feedback on the effects of what you are observing, whether it is passive resistance, active resistance, or serious aggression. Use your problem-solving skills to help the person understand the cause of the problem and search for solutions with you.

Manager sits down with colleague and uses open questions to discover her deeper objections to the plan

Unhappy about plans to change working procedures in her department, angry team member confronts manager

Manager is frustrated that team member is being difficult and fails to probe for the real reasons for her behaviour

91 Suggest how someone can take a more positive approach.

▼ **RESOLVING CONFLICT**
This scenario shows two possible outcomes. By working through conflict effectively, the manager improves his working relationship with the previously difficult team member. A failure to resolve the conflict leads to the loss of a valuable team member.

ADMITTING THAT PROBLEMS EXIST

You will be unable to move forwards together until both of you admit that problems exist. If the difficult person cannot see that there are issues, you must give feedback and ask questions until they can. It is unlikely that the team member will make a commitment to solving the problem until he or she can see the impact it is having on the objectives of the team, on the organization, or on the customers. Use open questions to explore what caused the problem and who else might be involved.

92 Keep an open mind – you may not be aware of the facts.

EXPLORING TOGETHER

Ask questions that pinpoint the real causes of the problem, then generate ideas to solve it. Ask the person to summarize the actions agreed between you to put the problem right. This allows you to check the person's understanding of the actions needed and his or her commitment to seeing them through. Exploring problems as they arise, and agreeing on actions, starts a more positive way of working together. Exploring your complementary strengths and weaknesses will help you build on this further.

Manager discovers that employee doubts her ability to meet new targets when plan is implemented

Together they explore ways to help employee meet new targets

Stressed employee fails to meet new targets when plan is imposed and decides to leave the organization

93 Steer discussions to future actions as opposed to past.

94 Acknowledge other people's points of view.

MAKING REQUESTS

If you tell people what to do, some people will do as directed. If you suggest what to do, twice as many people are likely to do what you want. Make your needs clear. Be direct and keep it short. Give the reason why you are asking, without trying too hard to sell the idea. Resist appealing to the person's emotions or using flattery. Respect the person's right to say "No". Put your energy into solving the problem and floating other suggestions rather than begging the person to say "Yes".

EXPRESSING YOUR VIEWS

Disagreements happen, but if you can express your views assertively, they are more likely to be handled constructively by a difficult person. Use logic and facts, and express your own opinions and feelings if you want to influence the person assertively. Suggest proposals that are positive and forward-looking and that start discussions moving. Say what you think or feel and use "I" more than "You" when giving your views. If you disagree with the person, then state this in a constructive way. First state what you agree with, then, in the same matter-of-fact way, state the reasons why you disagree with the other views or suggestions before moving on to say what you would like.

POINTS TO REMEMBER

● Making suggestions is more successful than telling difficult people what to do.

● By expressing disagreement assertively, you will help your team members to handle conflict constructively.

● A manager who means "No" needs to say so.

BEING ▶
ASSERTIVE
By expressing your opinions in an assertive, constructive way, you encourage a more assertive response from a previously nervous or defensive person. Make sure that you recognize their views while suggesting your own.

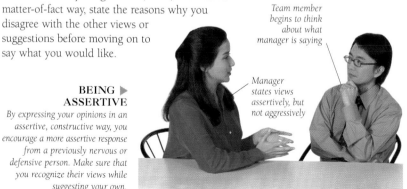

Team member begins to think about what manager is saying

Manager states views assertively, but not aggressively

SAYING "NO"

When you need to say "No", give the real reason for it. Avoid giving a long list of reasons or apologizing profusely for refusing. If the difficult person is persistent, repeat your reason for refusing rather than searching for a better one. Keep repeating the same message calmly and assertively until the person understands that you cannot change your decision: "I am happy to review the situation again in six months. What I cannot do is change the decision. We can arrange a review in mid-April". Eventually even the most aggressively persistent and difficult person will get the message, even if he or she does not like it.

95 Ensure that you show respect for others if you want it shown to you.

Team member tries to persuade manager to say "Yes"

Manager listens with open expression

GIVING WEIGHT ▶ TO A REFUSAL

When a difficult person is exhorting you to say "Yes", listen with an open expression and maintain good eye contact to demonstrate your assertiveness. Speak calmly and factually when you say "No".

CASE STUDY

Sandra managed a lively team in a busy agency. The team worked and played hard and in return Sandra was flexible about time off. Recently Sandra felt that they were prioritizing their social lives above meeting deadlines. Having stayed late several times to finish urgent jobs for clients, she felt angry that tasks had been left for her to complete. Sandra called a team meeting and calmly and assertively stated how she felt

about the team's behaviour. She explained that in taking on their work, her own work had not been completed on time, putting potential new business at risk. Sandra asked the team for ideas to solve the problem. They all agreed that with privileges on time off came responsibilities for seeing jobs through. Sandra was able to complete her own work and rely on her team to take their responsibilities seriously.

◀ RESOLVING CONFLICT

By stating how her team's behaviour had affected her, explaining what she wanted to happen instead, and exploring ideas to overcome the problem, Sandra helped her staff to appreciate how she felt and accept the facts. After this session, thinking ahead and ensuring that nothing was left for Sandra again became a matter of pride with the team.

USING MEDIATION

If the situation with a difficult person has become too stressful and time-consuming to deal with yourself, then using mediation can be a cost-effective option. A mediator has a responsibility to be impartial and neutral to help you both to reach agreement.

96 View involving a third party as a positive step, not a failing.

97 Talk through areas of disagreement constructively.

USING A MEDIATOR ▼
The mediator is someone whom the manager and team member trust. She hears both sides, and helps both people to analyze the problem. She may put an opposite point of view to both parties, while still commanding respect and trust.

HEARING BOTH SIDES

A mediator could be someone inside your organization who will listen and take a balanced view, and who has the sensitivity, maturity, and integrity to carry out this difficult role. If there is any chance that either you or the difficult person may doubt the neutrality of the mediator, engage an external mediator or consultant whom you are both confident will be impartial. The mediator will be present to manage the emotions and tension in a difficult situation constructively and to help you to listen to each other.

Mediator's body language is neutral

Difficult person trusts the mediator's impartiality

Manager states his views and what he hopes to achieve

SELECTING A MEDIATOR

Decide on the results you want to achieve from the process

Look at mediators with relevant training and experience

Ensure that mediator is someone whom the other party will respect and trust

Check the time limit and budget for the style of mediation chosen

RESOLVING THE ISSUES

A good mediator provides a means for resolving issues between you, and enables you both to retain a sense of control by being actively involved in decision-making. In very difficult situations, perhaps between customers or stakeholders in a contract, two mediators may be needed, one for each side. The outcome of mediation is never imposed on either party, so that both sides voluntarily enter into an agreement, feeling fully informed and heard. The agreement is more likely to be followed through if both parties have been actively involved in framing it. This is because no one will be left feeling aggrieved that a solution was imposed.

98 Find out whether a mediator needs both parties to describe the situation in writing before meeting.

DRAWING UP THE AGREEMENT

Before you start mediation, think about the results you want from the process. These should form the framework for the mediation and your agreement with the mediator. When you are selecting possible mediators, ask about their training and experience. Think about the kinds of skills, values, and style you expect. If issues exist between teams or departments, or between individual employees within an organization, the resulting agreement is usually psychological, written but not legally enforceable. Between customers and organizations, however, mediation to resolve disputes can lead to agreements that are legally enforceable.

CULTURAL DIFFERENCES

It is important to recognize that mediating between people of different cultures and backgrounds can be more difficult because of language barriers and misunderstanding of cultural nuances. If it is important to either party that they have someone of their own race, sex, or culture present, then this should be considered.

LEARNING FOR THE NEXT TIME

*E*very time you come into conflict with a difficult person, you can learn how to handle the situation better for next time. To develop your skill at dealing with difficult people, review how conflict arose in the first place, and how co-operation was gained.

99 Review what went well and what skills you must develop for next time.

QUESTIONS TO ASK YOURSELF

Q Did I listen? How many of my questions were open?

Q Was my behaviour assertive throughout?

Q Did I achieve an action plan from the difficult team member?

Q Did I let the team member summarize their own actions?

Q Have we arranged future sessions to review progress?

REVIEWING DEVELOPMENT AREAS

It is important to review yourself critically after every confrontation with a difficult person to see if you can identify your strengths and any areas that need development. Ask yourself questions about your performance, and make a list of any aspects that you would like to improve for the next time. Were you focused on the result you wanted? If not, set yourself a learning objective for the next time you confront a difficult person so that you will be clearer about what you want to change in yourself.

INVOLVING THE DIFFICULT PERSON IN REVIEWS

When you have worked with a difficult person over a period of time, review how you are working together. Ask for and give specific positive feedback on your working relationship and also on what you feel needs to change or be developed. Praise the behaviour you want repeated and give feedback on what you hope will change. Agree a ground rule that you should both give twice as much motivational feedback as developmental feedback.

100 Praise good behaviour that you would like to see repeated.

64

CREATING YOUR DEVELOPMENT PLAN

Reviews give you an opportunity to create a development plan for yourself. Identify the strengths you use with difficult people that you need to build on with practice. Look at the skills you need to develop, and decide whether practice alone will achieve the learning objectives you have set yourself, or whether you need training. Note what you want to be able to do and how well by the end of your next practice or training course.

POINTS TO REMEMBER

● Whether results are better or worse than expected, the reasons for both should be explored.

● Time should be taken to reflect on and celebrate successes.

● Everyone you work with should be encouraged to learn through regular reviews.

PERSONAL DEVELOPMENT PLAN

Name: BARRY TURNER

What	When	How	Results
To improve my observation and interpersonal skills to negotiate and communicate more effectively with difficult people at work	August	Training workshop (2 days) on communication and negotiation skills to be provided by external training provider Value: £850	● Learned to observe body language and my effect on others ● Performance improved as a result of using negotiation and assertiveness techniques to reach agreements with difficult people

Define needs plus outcomes you expect from training

Plan the best time for development activity or training

Describe cost of activity or training, duration, and provider

Record outcomes achieved from training or activity once completed

▲ DOCUMENTING DEVELOPMENT

You can encourage difficult people to create a Personal Development Plan for themselves and you can draw one up for yourself too. Include results as well as aims.

101 Agree on what you could both do better next time.

CREATING A JOINT DEVELOPMENT PLAN

If you have involved the difficult person in building the working relationship between you in reviews, you can both reflect on your achievements and identify your strengths as you build confidence in each other. You can also use reviews to recognize and plan further joint development needs and to improve your performance continuously. You will be surprised, in time, that you have changed your view about the difficult person you knew before.

ASSESSING YOUR ABILITY

A good knowledge of techniques to anticipate and manage difficult people is essential if you are to achieve consistently excellent performance from your staff. Test your skills by answering the following questions. If your answer is "Never" mark option 1; if it is "Always" mark option 4, and so on. Add your scores together, and refer to the analysis to see how you fared and to identify areas that need improving.

OPTIONS

1 Never

2 Occasionally

3 Frequently

4 Always

1 I know my staff well and understand what motivates them.

| 1 | 2 | 3 | 4 |

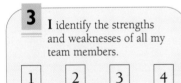

2 I observe my team members and monitor their workloads.

| 1 | 2 | 3 | 4 |

3 I identify the strengths and weaknesses of all my team members.

| 1 | 2 | 3 | 4 |

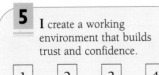

4 I understand that people have different ways of learning.

| 1 | 2 | 3 | 4 |

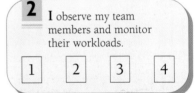

5 I create a working environment that builds trust and confidence.

| 1 | 2 | 3 | 4 |

6 I set measurable objectives with realistic timescales for achievement.

| 1 | 2 | 3 | 4 |

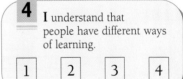

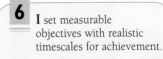

7 I greet all the people with whom I work and go on walkabouts daily.

1   2   3   4

8 I encourage staff to give feedback both to me and to each other.

1   2   3   4

9 I share information with my team and check their understanding.

1   2   3   4

10 I encourage people to focus on internal and external customer needs.

1   2   3   4

11 I ensure that everyone understands what is expected of them.

1   2   3   4

12 I understand my own strengths and weaknesses and plan my development.

1   2   3   4

13 I define a problem and plan how to overcome it by looking at several options.

1   2   3   4

14 I give myself time to think and prepare before meeting with difficult people.

1   2   3   4

15 I am assertive, and not passive or aggressive.

1   2   3   4

16 I always listen carefully to others.

1   2   3   4

17 I encourage people to move forwards rather than dwell in the past.

1　2　3　4

18 I identify reasons why people are unwilling to accept change.

1　2　3　4

19 I know when to confront difficult people and when to avoid confrontation.

1　2　3　4

20 I observe body language to give me advance warning of problems.

1　2　3　4

21 I know how to overcome objections to my suggestions.

1　2　3　4

22 I always follow up on actions agreed.

1　2　3　4

23 I set consistently fair objectives and standards for team members.

1　2　3　4

24 I give feedback on what behaviour should continue and what needs to change.

1　2　3　4

25 I evaluate information carefully and am aware of my own biases.

1　2　3　4

26 I ask open questions and listen more than I speak.

1　2　3　4

27 I know when someone is committed to taking action.

1   2   3   4

28 I know when to be flexible and when to hold my ground.

1   2   3   4

29 I summarize or ask the other person to summarize actions agreed.

1   2   3   4

30 I identify activities, roles, resources, and deadlines for milestones in my plans.

1   2   3   4

31 I can empathize with others while remaining objective.

1   2   3   4

32 I praise achievements and celebrate success with my team.

1   2   3   4

ANALYSIS

Now that you have completed the self-assessment, add up your total score and check your performance. Whatever level of success you have achieved, there is always room for improvement. Identify your weakest areas, then refer to the relevant sections of this book, where you will find practical advice and tips to help you establish and hone your skills.

32–63: You may still be surprised by difficult people. Practise your observation skills and give yourself time to prepare to handle difficult people more effectively.

64–95: You are aware of how to deal with difficult people in some more familiar situations but need to identify areas for further development.

96–128: You are able to achieve considerable success with difficult people. Develop your skills by asking for regular feedback.

INDEX

ACKNOWLEDGMENTS

AUTHOR'S ACKNOWLEDGMENTS

I would like to thank everyone who helped on this book, including Adèle Hayward, Amy Corzine, and Alison Bolus at Dorling Kindersley, and Mandy Lebentz, Arthur Brown, Peter Cooling, and Tish Mills at Cooling Brown.

PUBLISHER'S ACKNOWLEDGMENTS

Dorling Kindersley would like to thank the following for their help and participation in producing this book:

Photographers Matthew Ward, Steve Gorton

Models David Adkins, Tracey Allanson, Roger Andre, Phil Argent, Dale Buckton, Angela Cameron, Céline Cordwell, Lorraine Davies, Sander de Groot, Richard Hill, Cornell John, Aziz Khan, Michael Labat, Janey Madlani, Sophie Millett, Roger Mundy, Karen Murray, Kaz Takabatake, Suki Tan, Peter Taylor.

Make-up Janice Tee.

Picture research Franziska Marking.
Picture librarians Neale Chamberlain, Melanie Simmonds, Lee Thompson.

Indexer Hilary Bird.

PICTURE CREDITS

Key: *a* above, *b* bottom, *c* centre, *l* left, *r* right, *t* top
Corbis Stock Market: Jose L. Palaez 50; **Pictor International:** Robert Llewellyn 14;
gettyone stone: Christopher Bissell 4-5.
Jacket: Eyewire – front *cl*.

AUTHOR'S BIOGRAPHY

Christina Osborne is chief executive of Business Solutions, a strategic human resources consultancy, and advises private and public sector clients on designing organizations and developing people to succeed. Her executive director roles have spanned personnel, marketing, strategic business planning, and mergers and acquisitions. She has also held non-executive board roles in both public and private sectors. As a management consultant, she uses her facilitation and coaching skills to build effective teams. She has sat on industrial tribunals, has lectured in business schools, and is a Fellow of the Institute of Personnel and Development and the Institute of Directors in the UK.